Harrison Km P-7

Contents

Meet the Author

Meet the Illustrator

When **Norah Dooley** lived in Cambridge, Massachusetts, her neighbors came from many different countries. One day Norah decided to give a potluck dinner party. (At a potluck dinner, each guest brings something to eat.) When her guests arrived, five of them had brought rice dishes—all from different countries, and all delicious in their own special way. That gave Norah the idea to write *Everyone Cooks Rice*.

Like Norah Dooley, artist **Peter J. Thornton** used real people and places to bring the story *Everyone Cooks Rice* to life. Many of the pictures he created for the book show scenes from his own neighborhood in Providence, Rhode Island.

Everybody Cooks Rice

by Norah Dooley • illustrations by Peter J. Thornton

HOUGHTON MIFFLIN COMPANY

BOSTON

ATLANTA   DALLAS   GENEVA, ILLINOIS   PALO ALTO   PRINCETON

Acknowledgments

For each of the selections listed below, grateful acknowledgment is made for permission to excerpt and/or reprint original or copyrighted materials, as follows:

Selections

Everybody Cooks Rice, by Norah Dooley, illustrated by Peter J. Thornton. Copyright © 1991 by Carolrhoda Books, Inc. Reprinted by permission.

Photography

ii Courtesy of Norah Dooley **ii** Courtesy of Peter Thornton (r) **32** Tony Arruza (mr) **33** Harold Sund/The Image Bank (tr) **34** Peter Turnley/Black Star **35** McConnell McNamara (tr) **36** Henry T. Kaiser/Uniphoto (tl) **37** Ken Biggs/Tony Stone Images (mr) **38** Kevin A. Morris/Tony Stone Images (tl)

Houghton Mifflin Edition, 1996
Copyright © 1996 by Houghton Mifflin Company. All rights reserved.

Printed in the U.S.A.

ISBN: 0-395-73233-6

3456789-B-99 98 97 96 95

The artist would like to extend special thanks to his international cast of models.

To my families, immediate and extended, and with thanks to JED.
—N.D.

For Barbara
—P.J.T.

My stomach was grumbling. Mom was cooking dinner, and I couldn't wait to sit down and eat. "Carrie, will you go out and find Anthony—dinner is almost ready."

Mom is always asking me to look for Anthony. He's my little brother, and he's such a moocher! If he's not playing ball or hopscotch, he's at a neighbor's house tasting their dinner.

I walked outside and looked up and down the street. I couldn't see Anthony anywhere, so I went over to Mrs. Darlington's house. Anthony and I call her Mrs. D. She's our next-door neighbor.

7

Mr. and Mrs. D. are from Barbados. It was Thursday, so their grandchildren, Sean and Stephanie, were over having their favorite dinner—black-eyed peas and rice. At the front door I could smell fried onions and bacon. It made my mouth water. I ate a small cup of rice and black-eyed peas while Mr. D. told stories about Barbados. People swim there and go fishing—even in December!

Suddenly I remembered I was supposed to be looking for Anthony, so I asked if anyone had seen him. Sean said he'd seen Anthony going into the Diazes' house. I went there next.

9

When I walked into the kitchen, my friend Fendra Diaz and her little brother, Tito, were cooking dinner because their mom was working late. Tito was telling Fendra that she uses too much spice. Fendra said Tito was checking the pot too often, so the rice and pigeon peas would never cook. Their teenage brother, José, told them to pipe down. He wanted to watch TV.

I looked in the pot to see what was cooking. The rice was bright yellow! Fendra told me that her grandmother in Puerto Rico had taught her how to cook with turmeric. Turmeric makes rice yellow. Tito gave me a taste from the cooking spoon. Boy, was it delicious! Then I asked if anyone had seen Anthony. Fendra said Anthony had been there to taste their dinner but had left to visit Dong. So I went across the street to Dong's house.

Dong Tran came from Vietnam five years ago with his whole family—aunts, uncles, cousins, and all. Dong's older sister, Tam, answered the door. Mr. and Mrs. Tran work late every day, so everyone else takes turns making dinner. It was Tam's turn to cook. She was busy making the garlicky, fishy sauce, called *nuoc cham*. She let me try it on some rice. It was sweet and salty and sour. It tasted . . . interesting. Later when Mrs. Tran gets home, she'll make fried rice with peas. Then when Mr. Tran gets home, everyone will sit down and eat together.

When I asked if anyone had seen my brother, Dong said Anthony had been helping Mrs. Hua and Mei-Li with their groceries. The Huas live on the corner so I started to walk up the street.

"Carrie, wait up!" someone called. It was my friend Rajit. He was carrying three round metal boxes all clipped together. Something inside smelled delicious, so I asked him what it was. Rajit said his parents were working at their video and gift shop, so he was bringing them leftovers in a tiffin carrier.

There was a big party at the Krishnamurthys' house last weekend, so Rajit's mother cooked a fancy, colorful Indian dish called *biryani*. It's made with peas, cashews, raisins, lots of spices, and a special kind of rice called basmati rice. I had tasted *biryani* at Rajit's house the last time I went out looking for Anthony.

When I told Rajit that I was looking for my brother *again*, he said Anthony and Mei-Li were blowing bubbles out a window of the Huas' house.

The Huas came from China a year ago. Mrs. Hua is just learning how to speak English. We smile at each other a lot.

Mrs. Hua was steaming white rice for her family and the boarder who lives in the back room. She was also making tofu and vegetables in the wok— that's a big pan with a round bottom. Mrs. Hua always makes me sit down and eat something when I come over.

Everyone at the Huas' house uses chopsticks. Mei-Li, who is only three and a half years old, can even pick up a single grain of rice with her chopsticks! Mei-Li laughed at me when I tried using chopsticks and dropped some vegetables. She said Anthony was "bye-bye," so I decided to try our backyard neighbors, the Bleus.

The Bleus are from Haiti. Their cat just had kittens, so Anthony wanders over there a lot. Mrs. Bleu teaches English at the community center. We get to call her Madame Bleu. Madame Bleu speaks three languages—French, English, and Creole.

When I walked in, Madame Bleu was making a creole style Haitian dinner. It had hot peppers, chives, red beans, and you guessed it—rice. Monsieur Bleu works two jobs, so he won't get home till late. Madame Bleu says the pot will stay on the stove, and the rice will get tastier and spicier.

Adeline and Jeanne-Marie Bleu came home for dinner on their break from their after-school jobs at the grocery store. They helped themselves to bowls of rice and beans from the pot, and gave some to me. I thought my mouth was on fire! Jeanne-Marie teased me when I gulped some water.

It was getting late, and I still hadn't found Anthony. Adeline said she had seen him with a kitten in his arms, climbing the fence to our yard. I said thanks and *au revoir*—that means good-bye—and hurried home.

When I walked into the house, Anthony was showing the kitten to our baby sister, Anna. He was explaining to Mom that he was only borrowing the kitten.

Mom was putting dinner on the table. Her grandmother, from northern Italy, taught our grandmother, who taught Mom how to cook *risi e bisi*—rice with green peas. Mom puts butter, grated cheese, and some nutmeg on it. It smelled so good, but my stomach wasn't grumbling anymore. I told Mom that I was too full to eat. Anthony said he wanted to eat his dinner, even though he was full, because he loves rice, and that afternoon he found out that *everybody* cooks rice.

Rice

  2 cups rice
2½ cups water

1. Bring rice and water to a boil over high heat in a large covered saucepan.
2. Turn heat down to low and let rice simmer for 25 minutes or until all the water is absorbed.
3. Remove from heat and let stand for 10 minutes.
Note: This is a general rice recipe. Cooking instructions vary depending on type of rice used.

Mrs. D's Black-eyed Peas and Rice

  2 cups dried black-eyed peas
water
¼ cup vegetable oil
1 medium onion, peeled and chopped
2 slices bacon
1 teaspoon dried thyme
4 cups cooked rice
salt and black pepper to taste

1. Place black-eyed peas in a medium bowl and cover with cold water. Soak overnight.
2. Drain the peas, rinse, then boil in water for 20 minutes or until the black-eyed peas are tender. Drain and rinse the peas.
3. In a Dutch oven, heat the oil over medium heat, and sauté the onion and bacon. Break the bacon into small pieces.
4. Add thyme and stir.
5. Add cooked rice, black-eyed peas, salt, and pepper, stirring thoroughly to mix the ingredients.

The Diazes' Turmeric Rice with Pigeon Peas

1 vegetable or chicken bouillon cube
8 cups water
¼ cup cooking oil
1 green onion, finely chopped
½ teaspoon turmeric
4 cups cooked white rice
1 pound dried pigeon peas, soaked overnight
  and drained

Use a pot with a tight cover.

1. Dissolve bouillon cube in 1 cup water, then add
to the rest of the water. Set aside.
2. In the pot, combine oil, onion, and turmeric, and
cook over medium heat until onion is transparent.
Turn the heat off right away.
3. Add rice and water with dissolved boullion cube,
and cook for 10 minutes on the highest heat.
4. Lower the heat to medium and add the pigeon
peas. Stir a bit and cover.
5. Cook for about 15 minutes or until all the water
is gone.

Tam's Nuoc Cham

*Fish sauce can be found in any oriental market or the
international section of a supermarket.*

In a jar combine:
5 tablespoons fish sauce
2 tablespoons lime juice or 4 tablespoons white
  vinegar
1 peeled and finely grated carrot
3 cloves garlic, peeled and finely chopped or pressed
1 teaspoon crushed red pepper
1 to 1½ cups water
3 tablespoons sugar

1. Cover the jar and shake until the sugar is dissolved.
Note: *Nuoc cham* is used as a dip or a sauce and is
usually a part of every Vietnamese meal.

Mrs. Tran's Fried Rice

2 eggs
1 tablespoon butter
1 small onion, peeled and finely chopped
3 tablespoons oil
½ cup green peas
½ cup corn
1 carrot, peeled and grated
1 teaspoon sugar
1 tablespoon fish sauce
2 tablespoons soy sauce
4 cups cold cooked rice

1. Scramble the eggs in butter and set aside.
2. In a wok or large frying pan over medium heat, sauté onion in oil until it's transparent.
3. Add the vegetables and cook, stirring, for three minutes.
4. Add sugar, fish sauce, and soy sauce, and mix well.
5. Add rice and cook for about five minutes, stirring frequently, until all the food is hot.
6. Chop up the scrambled eggs, mix them in, and serve.

Rajit's Biryani

Basmati rice has a special flavor, but any sort of rice will do in a pinch. There should be at least two times as many vegetables and nuts as rice.

2 medium onions, peeled and chopped
2 tablespoons butter
Spices:
    2 cloves garlic, peeled and finely chopped
    2 teaspoons grated fresh ginger
    1 teaspoon ground coriander
    ¼ teaspoon each crushed black pepper, cayenne
      pepper, ground cloves, ground cinnamon,
      ground cardamom
    1 teaspoon cumin
Vegetables:
    ½ cup carrots, peeled and thinly sliced
    2 fresh tomatoes, peeled, quartered, and diced
    1 cup cauliflower florets
    1 cup green beans
    1 cup green peas
3 cups half-cooked rice (rice that has cooked for
   7 to 10 minutes)

2 tablespoons water
½ cup cashews or blanched almonds
½ cup raisins
2 hard-boiled eggs, peeled

1. In a large frying pan over medium heat, sauté onions in 1 tablespoon butter until golden.
2. Add all spices.
3. Add all the vegetables and sauté for 2 or 3 minutes.
4. Butter a large casserole dish and add all the ingredients, mixing or layering rice and vegetables.
5. Bake at 300 degrees F for 30-35 minutes.
6. Sauté cashews and raisins in 1 tablespoon butter.
7. Crumble hard-boiled eggs.
8. When biryani is baked, sprinkle with cashews, raisins, and crumbled hard-boiled eggs.

Mrs. Hua's Tofu with Vegetables

1 pound tofu, cut into 1-inch cubes
1 tablespoon soy sauce
1 tablespoon oyster sauce
1 teaspoon sesame oil
1 teaspoon sugar
4 tablespoons vegetable oil
½ teaspoon salt
2 cups green beans, cut into 1-inch lengths
½ cup water chestnuts
½ cup sliced mushrooms

1. Combine tofu, soy sauce, oyster sauce, sesame oil, and sugar. Refrigerate for at least one hour.
2. Heat 2 tablespoons vegetable oil in a wok or high-sided frying pan. Add salt, green beans, water chestnuts, and mushrooms. Cook, stirring constantly, for about two minutes. Pour into a bowl.
3. Add 2 tablespoons vegetable oil to the same wok.
4. Add tofu mixture and stir constantly for about 5 minutes.
5. Return green bean mixture to the wok and mix thoroughly.
6. Serve with cooked rice.

Madame Bleu's Rice and Beans

1 cup red beans
water
½ cup oil
2 slices bacon
2 cloves garlic, peeled and finely chopped
¼ cup chopped parsley
¼ teaspoon cayenne pepper (or more if desired)
1 teaspoon thyme
1 tablespoon chopped chives
4 cups cooked white rice

1. Place red beans in a medium bowl and cover with cold water. Soak overnight.
2. Drain the beans, rinse, then boil in water for 20 minutes or until the beans are tender.
3. Drain the beans and set aside.
4. In a frying pan over medium heat, heat oil and sauté bacon until lightly browned. Break into small pieces.
5. Add garlic, parsley, cayenne pepper, thyme, and chives. Now add the beans and fry gently.
6. Stir bean mixture into the cooked rice. Sprinkle with fresh chives.

Great-Grandmother's Risi e Bisi

2 cubes vegetable or chicken bouillon
4 cups water
1 clove garlic, peeled and finely chopped
1 small onion, peeled and finely chopped
3 tablespoons olive oil
2 cups uncooked rice
2 cups fresh or frozen green peas
½ to 1 cup grated Parmesan cheese
½ teaspoon ground nutmeg

Use a pot with a tight cover.

1. In a bowl, dissolve bouillon cubes in 2 cups of water, then add to the rest of the water. Set aside.
2. Over medium heat, cook garlic and onion in olive oil until the onion is transparent. Don't let the garlic turn brown!
3. Turn off heat right away and pour in rice. Stir in the 4 cups of water and dissolved bouillon and cook on highest heat until mixture boils. Lower heat and do not remove lid. Cook for 25 minutes.
4. If using frozen peas, soak them in warm water. When rice is cooked, add peas, stir in Parmesan cheese, and sprinkle with nutmeg.

World Map

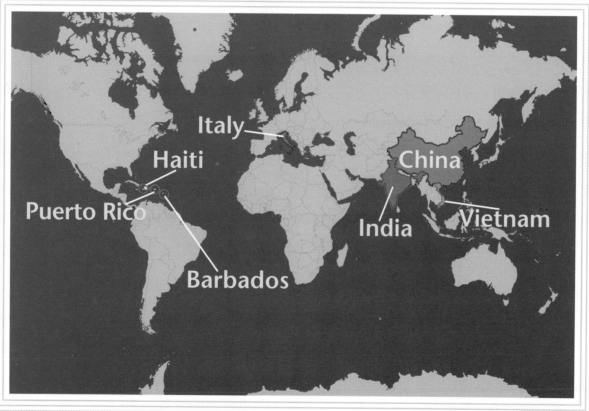

Italy
Haiti
Puerto Rico
Barbados
China
India
Vietnam

For a closer look at these seven countries, turn the page. →

Barbados

(an island nation in the Caribbean Sea)

Size: 166 square miles (about one-seventh the size of Rhode Island)

Number of people: 254,000

Climate: mainly mild and pleasant

Some important products: sugar, cotton, fish

Official language: English

Capital city: Bridgetown

FUN FACTS

The lovely climate of Barbados makes it a favorite vacation spot. The number of people who visit each year is twice the number of people who actually live there!

Steel bands create lively, rhythmic music in Barbados. The instruments are made from metal barrels that once contained oil.

The government of Barbados produces especially beautiful postage stamps, showing the island's colorful flowers, birds, and ocean wildlife.

BEIJING
CHINA

CHINA
(a country in Asia)

Size: 3,696,100 square miles (slightly larger than the United States)

Number of people: 1,169,619,000 (the largest population in the world)

Climate: Because of its size, China has many different climates.

Some important products: cloth, rice, tea, oil, coal, cattle, fish

Official language: Mandarin (Northern Chinese)

Capital city: Beijing

FUN FACTS

● One out of every five people in the world is Chinese.

Over 3,500 years ago, people in China discovered how to make silk cloth from the thread of the silkworm. They kept their secret from the rest of the world for hundreds of years.

To write English, you must learn how to form twenty-six different letters. To write Chinese, you must learn to draw thousands of different symbols.

HAITI

PORT-AU-PRINCE

Haiti

(an island nation in the Caribbean Sea)

Size: 10,579 square miles (about the size of Maryland)

Number of people: 6,431,000

Climate: hot and humid on the coast; cooler in the mountains

Some important products: coffee, sugar, bananas, cocoa, rice, cloth, bauxite
(a mineral used to make aluminum), cattle, goats

Official languages: French and Creole

Capital city: Port-au-Prince

FUN FACTS

● Haiti covers the western part of the island of Hispaniola. The rest of the island belongs to the Dominican Republic.

Most of Haiti is covered with mountains. Some Haitians farm such steep land that they must tie themselves to an anchor to keep from sliding down the slope.

Haitian farm workers often sing together and play music as they work. They call this combination of work and play a *combite*.

INDIA
(a country in Asia)

Size: 1,266,595 square miles (about one-third the size of the United States)

Number of people: 886,362,000 (the second largest population in the world)

Climate: Because of its size, India has many different climates.

Some important products: rice, wheat, mangoes, spices, timber, fish, iron, coal, diamonds, steel, cloth, electronic goods, jewelry, carpets

Official languages: Hindi and English

Capital city: New Delhi

During the wet season, known as the monsoon, 118 inches of rain may fall in the city of Bombay.

The game of chess was first played in India.

Elephants are a common sight in some parts of India. They sometimes even wander into people's yards and feast on their gardens!

ITALY

ITALY
(a country in Europe)

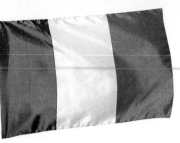

Size: 116,303 square miles (about the size of Georgia and Florida combined)

Number of people: 57,904,000

Climate: mainly warm and pleasant along the coast, colder in the mountains

Some important products: wheat, rice, grapes, olives, sheep, pigs, goats, cattle, fish, pasta, cars, clothing, chemicals, electronic goods

Official language: Italian

Capital city: Rome

FUN FACTS

● To cross the street in Venice, Italy, you need a boat. The "streets" are canals.

If you visit Italy, don't try to go shopping from about 1 to 4 P.M. Most businesses are closed in the afternoon (but they stay open until 8 in the evening).

The most familiar kind of pasta made in Italy is spaghetti, which means "little strings." But Italians make more than 500 other kinds of pasta.

Puerto Rico

(a self-governing island that is part of the United States)

Size: 3,427 square miles (about three-fourths the size of Connecticut)

Number of people: 3,580,332

Climate: warm and pleasant

Some important products: coffee, plantains, pineapples, bananas, sugarcane, pigs, chickens, lobsters, chemicals, clothing, leather goods

Official languages: Spanish and English

Capital city: San Juan

FUN FACTS

The national animal of Puerto Rico is a tiny frog called the coqui. Found only in Puerto Rico, it fills the night air with its clear, high song.

Roberto Clemente, one of the best all-around baseball players in history, was born in Carolina, Puerto Rico. A baseball stadium in Hato Rey was named after him.

Phosphorescent Bay, on the southwest coast of Puerto Rico, gives a light show every night. The waters are filled with tiny sea creatures that glow in the dark.

HANOI

VIETNAM

Vietnam
(a country in Asia)

Size: 127,330 square miles (about the size of New Mexico)

Number of people: 68,964,000

Climate: warm all year, with abundant rainfall

Some important products: rice, corn, sugar, rubber, cattle, pigs, fish, coal, iron, bauxite, cloth, cement, fertilizer

Official languages: Vietnamese (Chinese is also spoken.)

Capital city: Hanoi

FUN FACTS

To speak Vietnamese, you have to know not only how to pronounce the words but also what tone to use. Depending on the tone, the word *ma* can mean "but," "mother," "horse," "rice seedling," "tomb," or "ghost."

On their way to work, many Vietnamese people stop for a quick breakfast of noodle soup at one of the many food stalls that line the sidewalks.

In Vietnam, water puppet shows are performed outdoors in small ponds. The puppeteers stand waist-deep in the water and are hidden behind a screen.